RUBANK EDUCATIONAL LIBRARY No. 41

RUBANK

Elementary Method

SAXOPHONE

N. W. HOVEY

A FUNDAMENTAL COURSE FOR INDIVIDUAL OR LIKE-INSTRUMENT CLASS INSTRUCTION

RUBANK®

HAL•LEONARD® CORPORATION
7777 W. BLUEMOUND RD. P.O. BOX 13819 MILWAUKEE, WI 53213

LESSON 1

Whole Notes and Whole Rests

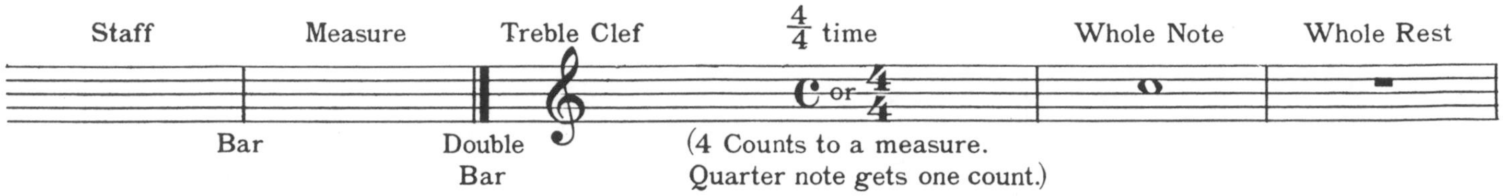

1

2

3

4

5
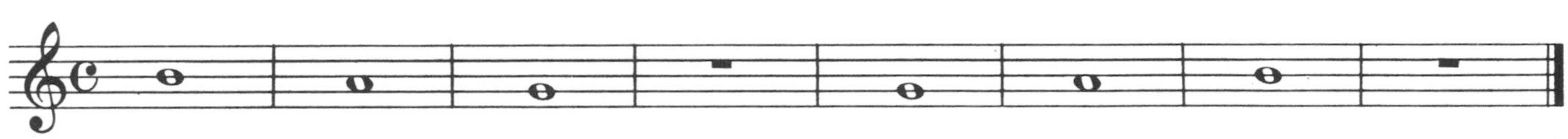

6

7
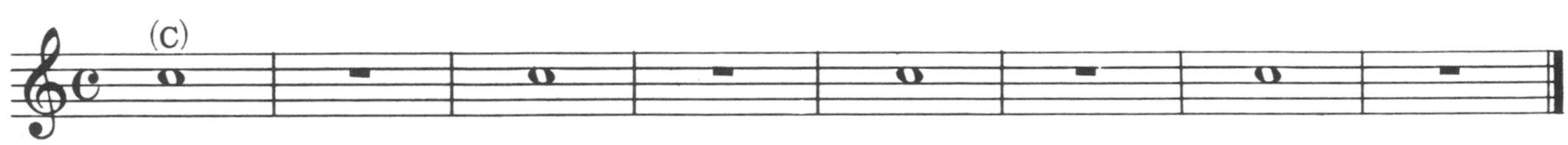

8

9

10
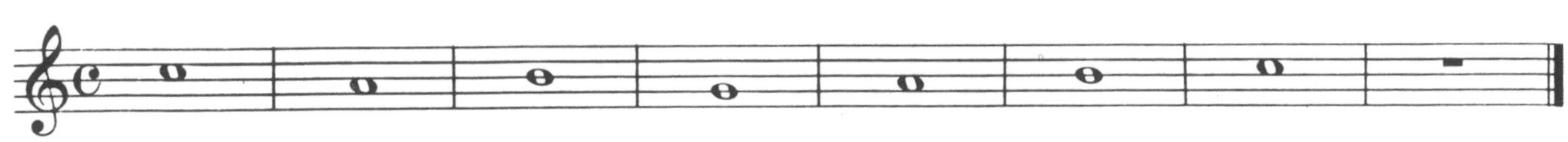

Half Notes and Half Rests

1 

2 

3 

4 

5 

6 

7 

8 

Duet

9 

Extending the Range

1 

2 

3 

4 

5 

6 

7 

8 

Also play no. 8 in half notes  etc.

9 

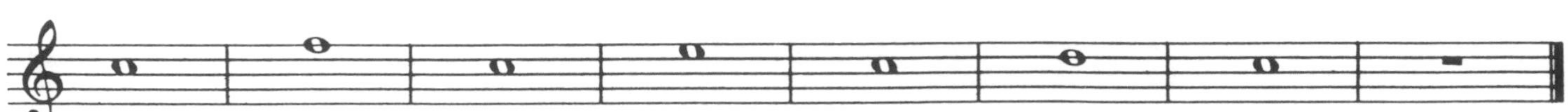

Also play no. 9 in half notes 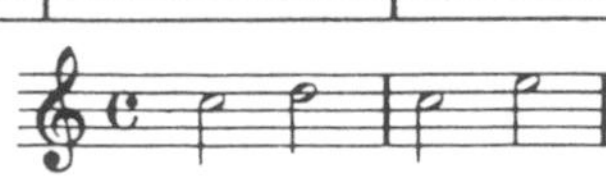 etc.

10 

Quarter Notes

1 

2 

3 

4 

5 

6 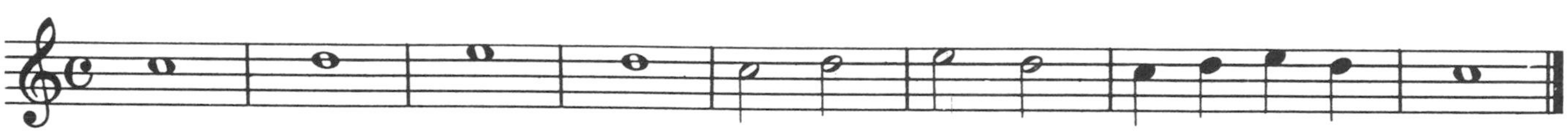

7 

8 

9 

10 

11 

*) The sign ⁒ indicates that the preceding measure is to be repeated.

Quarter Notes and Rests

1

3

4

5

6

Note: Check the pitch of the high "A" by playing octaves and listening carefully. A slight change in lip tension may be necessary.

Key of F

(one flat — B)
(B♭)

1 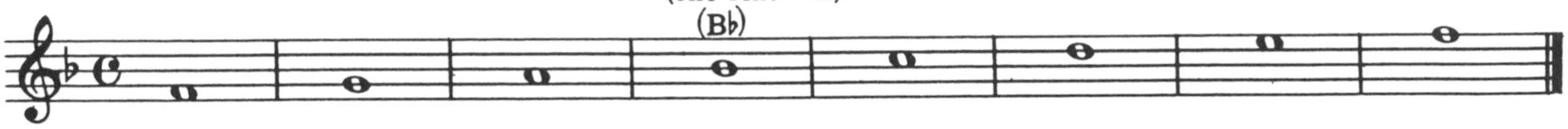

2 

3 

4 

5 

6 

2–4 time; two counts in a measure instead of four.

7 

Duet – Lightly Row

8 

The Tie; Dotted Half Notes

1

2

3

4

5

Duet

6

★) The sign ♮ is called a "natural". It cancels the effect of the B♭ in the key signature for one measure only. Occasional sharps, flats, or naturals not appearing in the key signature are called accidentals.

Three Quarter Time

1

2

3

Duet–German Waltz

4

5

Eighth Notes

Rhythmic patterns to be practiced. Repeat each several times.

1

2

Duet–Blue Bells of Scotland

3

4

5

Eighth Notes

1

2

Duet–Long Long Ago

3

D. S. is an abbreviation for Dal Segno which means "from the sign." Go back to the sign (𝄋) and play to *Fine* (end).

Slow–sustained–as even as possible in volume and pitch.

4

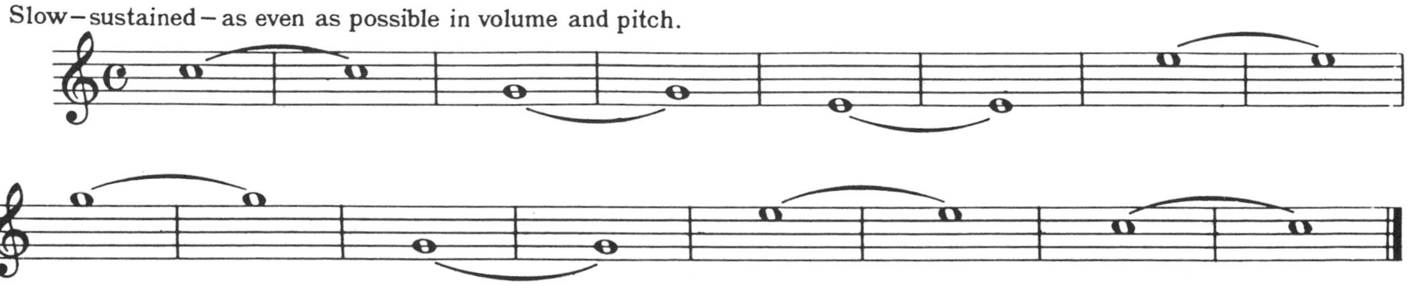

Eighth Notes

1

2

3

4

C major scale
(memorize)

F major scale
(memorize)

Review Lesson

for development of technique
(see footnote)

This page may be given as a single lesson or it may be assigned in parts, according to the ability of the pupil. No new problem is taken up at this point.

Key of G

(one sharp – F)

1

2

3

4

5

Duke Street

Moderato

6

7

G major scale
(memorize)

Before proceeding with lesson 14, be certain that you can recognize and define the key signatures that you have had thus far (namely, C, F and G) and that you have *memorized* three major scales.

Dotted Quarter Notes

Rhythmic patterns to be practiced. Repeat each several times.

1

2

3

Duet—In the Gloaming

A. F. HARRISON

4

Dotted Quarter Notes

1

Note time signature.

2

3

4

Slurs

Key of B♭

(two flats–B and E)

1
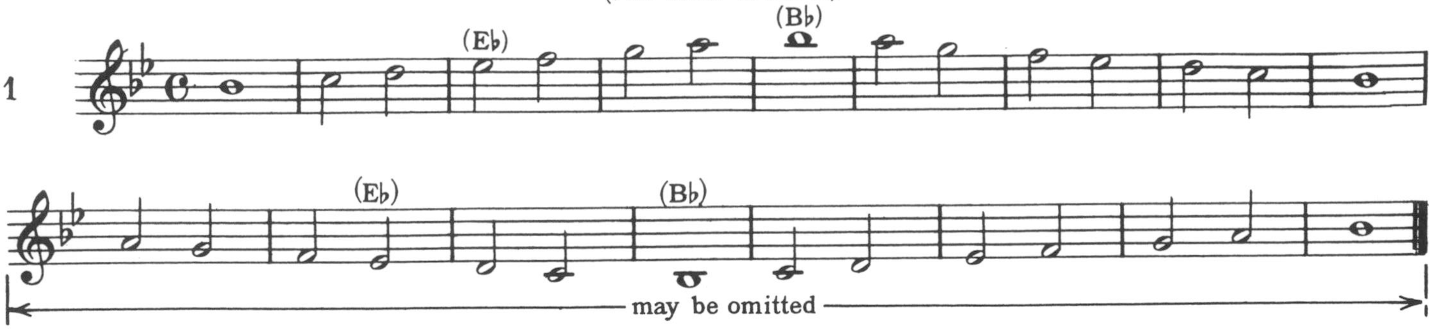

2

3

Trio to "Ambassador" March

DAVIS

4

5

★ Use correct B♭ fingering in major chord.

B♭ major scale (memorize)

Play four major scales from memory before proceeding with lesson 18.

Eighth Rests

Rhythmic patterns to be practiced. Repeat each several times.

Sixteenth Notes

(see footnote)

1 

2 

3 

4 

Accompaniment Rhythms

5 

Number 1 is a rhythmic exercise. Play both lines and compare. Notice that any eighth note may be replaced by two sixteenths. Invent some rhythmic patterns of your own.

Sixteenth Notes

1

2

3

4

Sixteenth Notes

1

2

3

4

Review no. 4 using these articulations:

Key of A

(three sharps—F, C, and G)

1 

2 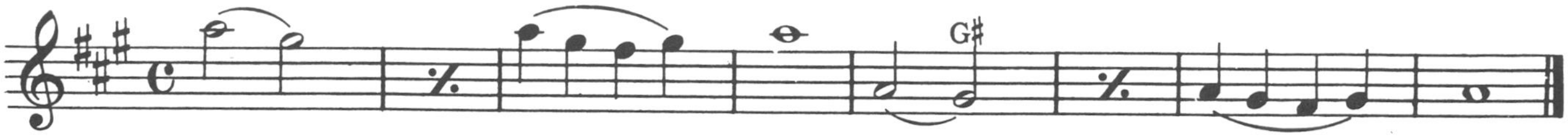

3 

4 

Sweet and Low

BARNBY

5 

A major scale
(memorize)

Play seven major scales from memory before proceeding with lesson 33

Dotted Eighths Followed by Sixteenths

1

2

3

4

Duet—Tramp, Tramp, Tramp

ROOT

5

Dotted Eighths Followed by Sixteenths

1

2

Trio — My Maryland

3

1st part
2nd part
3rd part

Additional Rhythms in Alla Breve

1

2

3

March

4

Review Lesson for Development of Technique

1

2

Key of A♭

(four flats — B E A and D)

1 

2 

3 

4 

5 

Melody

SCHUMANN

6 

A♭ major scale (memorize) 

Play eight major scales from memory before proceeding with lesson 38.

Syncopation

1
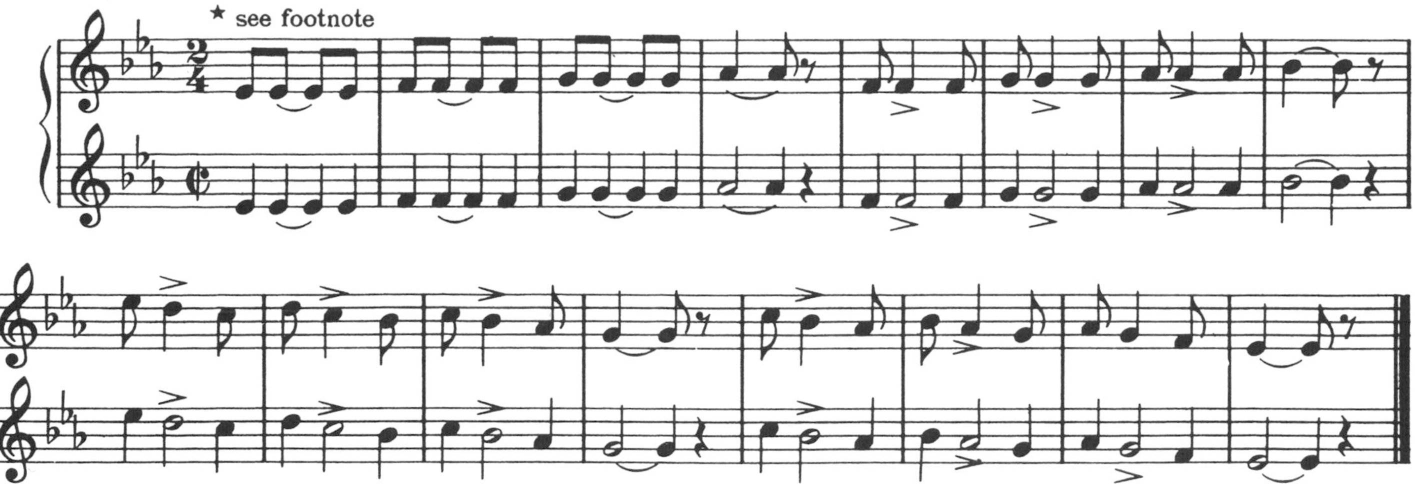

2

Old Folks at Home

FOSTER

3

Annie Laurie

Scotch Melody

4

Be certain the accent is on the correct note. A common error is committed by playing syncopated figures as follows:

Syncopation

1 2 3 4

Key of E

(four sharps—F, C, G and D)

1

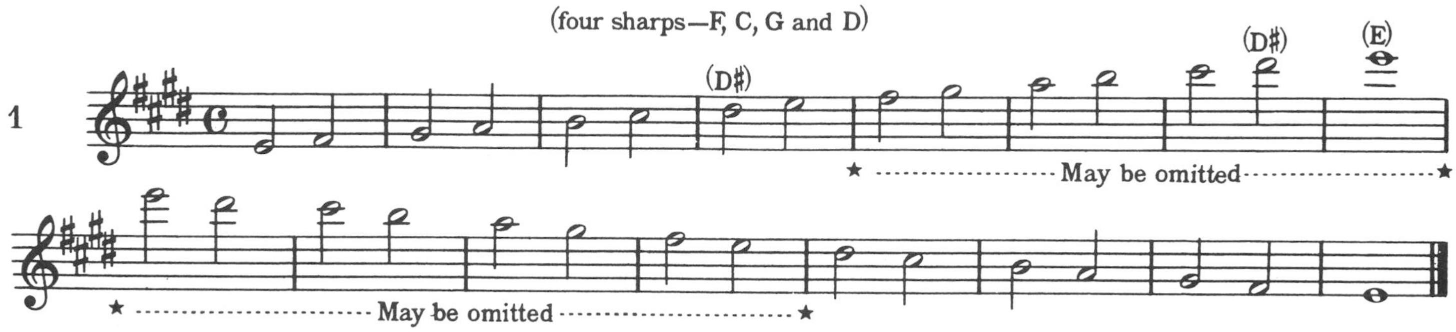

2

Technical Study

3

Hunter's Chorus

WEBER

4

E major scale (memorize)

Play nine major scales from memory before proceeding with lesson 41.

Chromatic

1

2

Chromatic

1

2

Waltz

3

Triplets

In previous lessons you have divided the quarter notes into two equal parts (♩= ♫) and into four equal parts (♩= ♬♬). It may also be divided into three equal parts: (♩= ♪♪♪ with 3).

1

2

3

4

Scenes That Are Brightest

WALLACE

5

Be certain you play each of the notes in the triplet figure with equal value. A common error is committed by playing the figure in this way: ♫♩. Do not rush the first two notes.

A Study on Construction of Major and Minor Scales

Example
"C major"

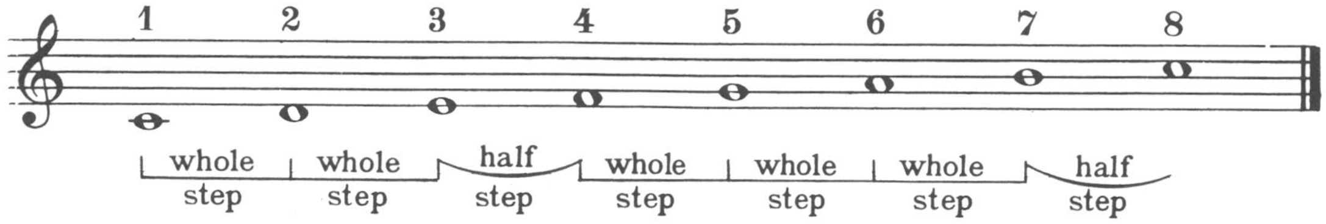

To be SPELLED correctly a scale must be on successive lines and spaces. Note HALF STEPS between 3rd and 4th degrees and 7th and 8th degrees.

Work out the following scales, then fill in correct key signature.

major

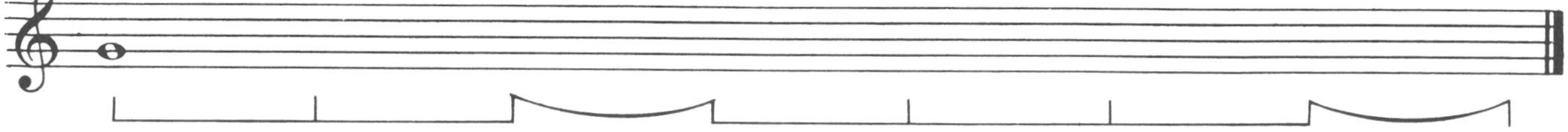

major

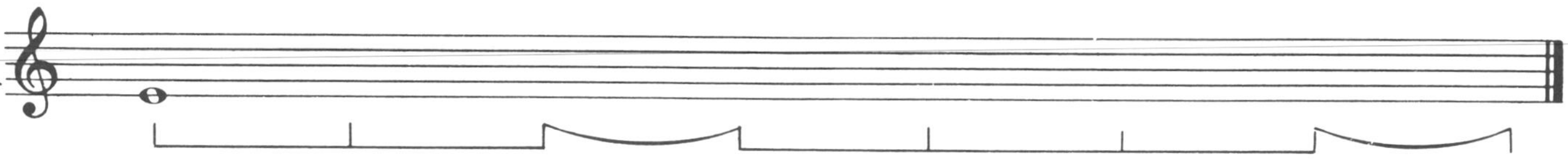

major

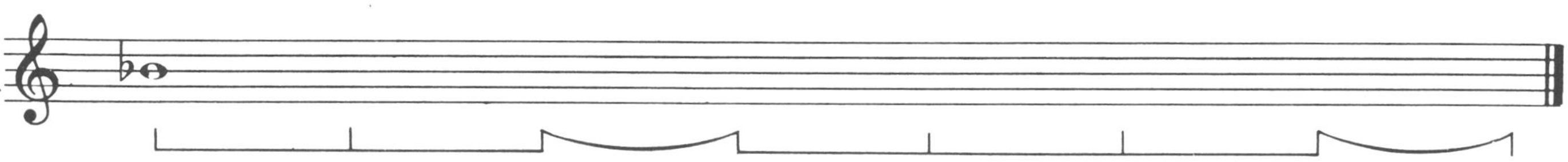

major

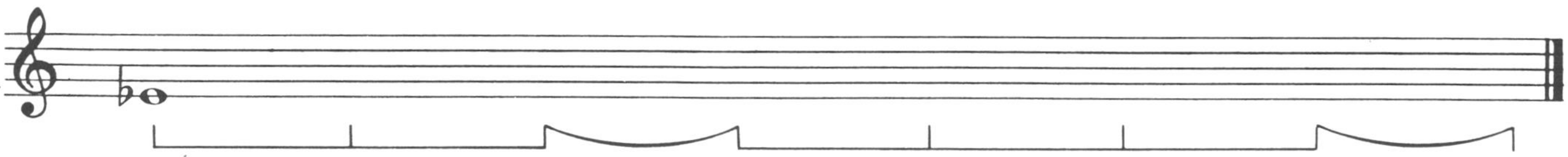

Example
"A minor"
(melodic)

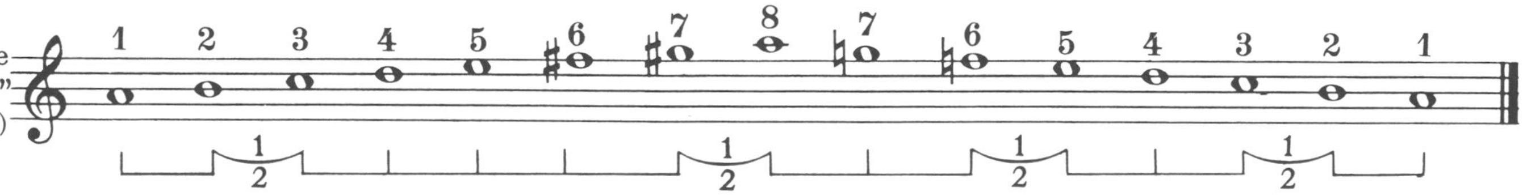

Note that the key signature is that of the RELATIVE MAJOR SCALE which starts on the third degree of the minor. In the above example (A minor) the key signature is the same as C major (called the RELATIVE MAJOR) which starts on the third degree of the A minor scale.

minor

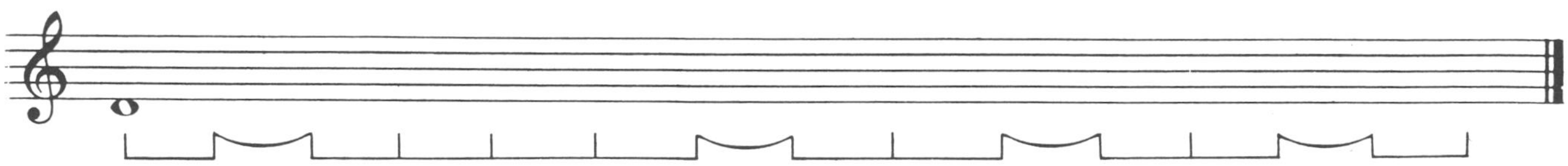

minor

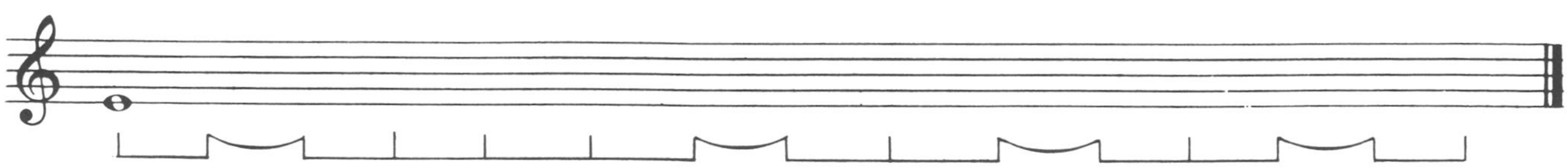

minor

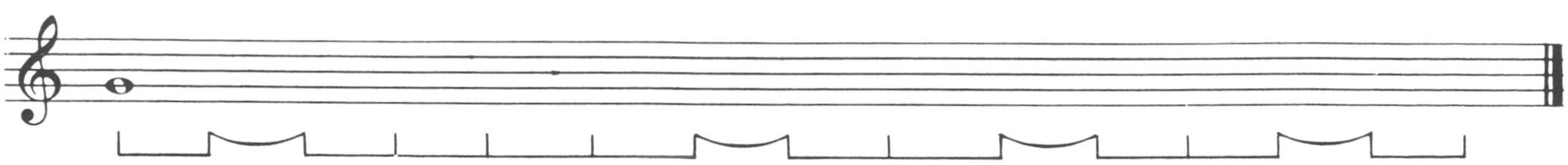

minor

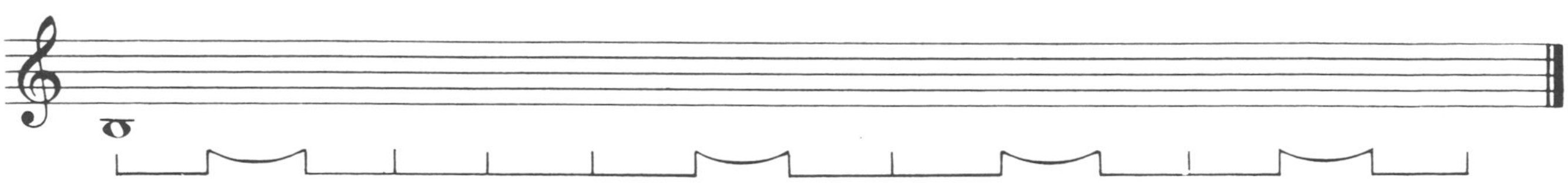

Major Scales for Reference

Common Minor Scales

Chromatic

Chord Studies